HEPROV

The Monologue Collection, Volume II

Akilah Logan

Published by Akilah Logan. 2018

While every precaution has been taken in the preparation of this book, the **pub**lisher assumes no responsibility for errors or omissions, or for damages resulting from the use of the information contained herein.

INPROV

First edition. August 6, 2018.

Copyright © 2018 Akilah Logan.

Written by Akilah Logan.

**It's okay for your to feel…It's actually preferred…
Do what is needed.**

FOREWORD

So many actors struggle with the idea of working a 9 to 5 to support themselves while pursuing their dreams. "*TO BE OR NOT TO BE*" an Actor?! That is the question. Here's the answer. If you are truly S.E.R.I.O.U.S about pursuing your dreams then it's important to support your dreams until your dreams can support you. So, with that said...Create a new way of thinking, create a new way of living, create a new way of being. I always encourage actors to ask three important questions when breaking down their scenes, and I strongly believe this applies to real life...to real people, to everyone.

Question #1: What Do I Want?
Question #2: What's Stopping Me From Getting What I Want?
Question #3: Who Am I?

Once you can answer these questions, you will solve your problem but only if you are truly honest with yourself.

Akilah and I met at my One On One Acting Class. We would meet once per week in my New Jersey office in Downtown Newark. Each week we would dive into Scene Work, Character Work and Emotional Work. We would apply my 3 rules to the monologue assigned the week before and each week it would be an eye-opening experience as she discovers the best way to utilize her acting tools. I always end each class with Akilah by saying "do you have any questions regarding our session?" She sometimes hesitates before she speaks but this one particular night she said she was struggling with moving, making money and being true to herself.

So, I asked her my three favorite questions, "What Do You Really Want? What's Stopping You From Getting What You Want? and Who Are You?" By the time we finished answering all three questions she was on the path to success.

Here's the deal, we are all given a Special Skill, Talent, A Gift... however you want to word it, whatever "it" is. It's there and here's how you recognize it. It's the first thing you think about when you wake up in the morning. It's the last thing you think about before you go to bed. It's the thing that wakes you up out of your sleep at night. It's your

PASSION. And its inside of you waiting to be unleashed. So, let it out and you can turn your dreams into a reality and that salary into a salary.

During our talk, I said to Akilah, "If you have a special skill or a hidden talent. Find a way to make money doing it. If you think it, Ink it. Create a plan and stick to it."

I discovered she's an amazing writer and a good story teller and as you know by now she's written monologue books for aspiring actors and actresses. This will allow her to support her dreams until her dreams can support her. Dream Big.

Wendy Mckenzie
Acting Coach / Creative

HEPROV: THE MONOLOGUE COLLECTION

Table of Contents

HEAR ME 12

I'LL BE BACK 13

THE DOUBLE STANDARD 15

GUILTY PARTY 17

BETRAYAL 19

REWIND THE TIME 21

CO-CRAZY 23

EVERYDAY PATHWAY 25

EXCEPT ANY OLE THING 27

LOVE WHO YOU LOVE 29

SO YOU THOUGHT 31

THE SACRIFICE 33

TOO LITTLE, TOO LATE 35

GONE TOO SOON 37

I'M READY 39

STANDING IN ATTENTION 41

HEPROV: THE MONOLOGUE COLLECTION

NO MORE BOY 43

PAUSE FOR A SECOND 45

ODDBALL 48

EQUAL WORK 49

OPENLY TOXIC 51

REVERSE ABUSE 54

SEE CLEARLY 55

JUDGE YE 58

PLACE THE BLAME 60

WE CAN'T HURT 62

ARE WE READY? 63

A DIFFERENT KIND 65

PAY THE PIPER 67

MY PRECIOUS 69

SHADOW NO MORE 71

TIME WASN'T OUR FRIEND 73

OPEN SESAME 75

TRUE REALITY 77

HEPROV: THE MONOLOGUE COLLECTION

IT'S NOT ALL OF US 79

WHEN IT HITS 81

ODE TO CHANGE 83

DOCILE 85

SAME TIME, SAME THING 87

LAPPY 89

CHAINS THAT BIND ME 91

IT AIN'T REAL 93

THE ONLY ONE 95

REMINISCE TO REVOLT 97

TIRED YET? 99

REMEMBERING YOUR PLACE 101

MAMA'S BOY BREAKUP 103

ROLE REVERSAL 106

HIDING 107

OLD FAMILY 109

HEPROV: THE MONOLOGUE COLLECTION

HEAR ME

So, I stand here,
Waiting for prayers to be answered
That I assume you heard.
Preacher always told me my life is in your Word.
But are we really sure?
Lately, I haven't been hearing or seeing what I've been believing for.
According to everyone else,
You have so much in store.
I took a leap of faith.
Steady grinding to make
Every possibility open
Fully knowing everything that's at stake.
So, I stand here,
Praying to a God that I think hears me but instead
I hear the fears of everyone else,
Telling me I'm a failure.
Do you hear me?
Do You?
Are you even here?
Last time I checked the loudest person I should be hearing is you.
Are you gonna talk?
Or just sit there
Watching me.
Do I need to do something stupid to get your attention?
Cause, I need you now.
And you're not answering.
I shouldn't have to hit rock bottom for you to save me.
People wonder why
I listen to my own anthem.

HEPROV: THE MONOLOGUE COLLECTION

I'll BE BACK

Sometimes I feel like a born failure.
I wake up with the weight of the world of my shoulders
Trying to make sure I don't die tonight.
It's plenty of people that wanna see me fail.
Just to say I told you so.
Some try to knock my hustle because I can't make time for them like I did before.
Making moves causes me to make new friends while the old ones stay the same.
Laughing cause I'm different.
And again, they remain.
Can't kick it with you like we used to
Truth be told, kickin with you never ends well.
It's a lot going on that I can't tell you.
Cause I know you won't understand.
You'll just laugh and say I ain't a man.
The lack of support adds pressure that none of you can endure.
Standing on my own two feet
Not something to abhor.
It's harder to go against the grain
Easier to be a statistic.
In order to continue on,
Your distance is my existence.
But don't worry, I'll never forget.
My fellow brother,
When I cast my net.

HEPROV: THE MONOLOGUE COLLECTION

THE DOUBLE STANDARD

How many times I gotta tell you,
They don't want you.
They only want parts of you.
To prove my love, I gotta do 50 million things to make you happy.
When all I ask is for you to be loyal.
Be loyal to my grind.
Be loyal to my journey.
You too busy looking at the next man
Drooling over what he got.
You think I don't want my own?
You think I don't wanna take you wherever you wanna go,
Whenever?
Nah, You want it now.
It's funny that you want me to be patient with your trust issues,
But I gotta be rich…for you…NOW?
Here is the double standard!
I didn't complain when you asked me 20 questions about my day.
Not because you cared but you wanted to see who I was with.
But if I can't take you to some dumb expensive restaurant then I'm not being the man you need.
What about when you were crying because you didn't get that promotion,
Who sat up all night with you?
Listening to you go on and on about how the system is broken because a man got it?
ME!
Or when YOUR car broke down,
Who drove in the middle of the night to pick you up?
Or when you were sick, and you threw up…RIGHT ON MY SHIRT.
Oh, but I forgot, that's my job…
So, tell me what's yours?

HEPROV: THE MONOLOGUE COLLECTION

HEPROV: THE MONOLOGUE COLLECTION

GUILTY PARTY

There are so many yes' and rarely any no's
When it comes to you.
But you don't notice.
You don't pay attention.
Every day, I get up with the expectation of what a man is supposed to be
Striving to handle every situation that meets me at the door.
But it's never enough.
When you think you've crossed the threshold,
It always someone right there to tell you there's more.
So, you know what I do?
MORE.
Forget the heartache.
Forget the pain.
Oh wait, I'm not supposed to feel that.
Right?
The minute I show an ounce of emotion, I'm weak.
I'm not a man,
I'm soft.
I walk around like a robot but when you cry and when you hurt,
That's when I'm "allowed" to flick it on.
For you.
You can't even imagine what I go through on a daily.
Cause you never asked.
And now when you see me talking to another woman you wanna throw on the guilt because you're not doing your job?
Nope.
I don't wanna hear it.
You didn't even ask who she was.
You allowed your guilty conscious to make up an entire story because you dropped the ball.
I'm not here to feed the insecurities that you failed to handle.
I don't complain when you need me because I love you.
But for someone you claim to love,
I have to beg for affection?

HEPROV: THE MONOLOGUE COLLECTION

BETRAYAL

You know,
I really thought I was falling in love with you.
You are everything that I knew I needed.
You're beautiful, Intelligent, Sarcastic.
I expected us to get along.
To move through life together.
What I didn't expect,
You sleeping with my best friend.
Lying about how it just happened.
One thing lead to another.
You hold men to such high standards that you can't even achieve yourself.
But I'm supposed to understand that you're a "free spirit"
Understand what your free spirit has cost you.
The person you wanted to be with.
There's no way you can expect me-
I can't even look you in the eye
You want me to move past this like we're this tight unit.
You crossed the line and fortunate for me,
I'm strong enough to deny you.
I know you didn't think so.
I'm some sappy dude that was "sweatin" you.
Handled my business like a man.
Wasn't out here messing with 4 different women
Bringing around drama.
You like that type of dude.
Those who really don't respect you.
They just only want you.
It's a shame you don't know the difference
When someone actually cares for you.

HEPROV: THE MONOLOGUE COLLECTION

REWIND THE TIME

I can't believe I told her I loved her.
It slipped out.
I mean, I like her but not like that.
She was crying and I was just trying to console her.
What am I gonna do?
Tell her I was just playing?
She will go crazy!
You know she's crazy right!
It all happened so fast!
(pause)
Who am I kidding.
I do love her.
I just didn't expect-.
To happen like this
She's cute and all but definitely not my usual type.
She's funny and doesn't take life so serious.
I just don't know how to make this work.
What does she really need me for?
She got her own money, own place.
She's pretty head strong, so arguments will be fun.
I'm still trying to own something.
I don't think this is gonna work.
Maybe we can somehow just be friends.
I mean I love my friends?
That'll give me some time.
To get myself together.
I'll just pretend it wasn't that serious.
Or, it never happened.

HEPROV: THE MONOLOGUE COLLECTION

CO-CRAZY

How do you maintain when your daughter's mother
IS CRAZY?
I provide for my daughter, pick her up from school.
Spend time with her as much as possible.
But it ain't enough.
ITS NEVER ENOUGH.
I never met someone so focused on making my life a living hell
Just because we are not together.
Never knew someone who deliberately tries to
Sabotage relationships.
Even work situations.
Why can't we just co parent like regular adults?
She gotta call me in the middle of the night,
During work,
When I'm out.
For stuff she can handle herself.
But who I am?
Just the father.
No matter what happens…Just deal with it.
And I know she talks bad about me.
Ask my daughter she'll tell you.
I ain't good enough, I'm a deadbeat.
There have been plenty of times she'll just drop my daughter off with
no warning.
Cause she wanna go out, have a life.
And I just gotta take it.
Now, don't get me wrong, I love my daughter.
But I do have a life that I would like to live.
To make enough to provide for her and maybe one day
get married.
I don't know. I can't even look down that road.
This woman just stresses me out.
Where's the reset button?

HEPROV: THE MONOLOGUE COLLECTION

HEPROV: THE MONOLOGUE COLLECTION

EVERYDAY PATHWAY

The pressures of being successful are already stacked up against me
But nobody pays attention to that.
Staying on the right path and keeping my nose clean is an everyday struggle.
Because the streets is easier.
You see me as an animal
So you treat me as such.
According to your mind,
I could never amount to anything besides
The joker you see.
When I try to elevate
You place your foot on my back
To prevent me from moving
The pursuit of happiness that you claim everyone is privy to…
But me.
I walk around with an X on my back
Waiting for the day,
I become the next hashtag.
Not because I've done wrong but because
You fear me.
You fear my strength, my stature
And the ability to rearrange
What society deems insane.
Like my education and my intellect.
To you, we will never be the same.
So you craft a narrative where I always lose
And you constantly win.
Not understanding that I will always find a way.
My success is not contingent upon the appearance of your wealth.
It is based on the cultivation
Of my own.

HEPROV: THE MONOLOGUE COLLECTION

EXCEPT ANY OLE THING

The blatant disrespect I get because I don't agree with
EVERYTHING you claim you want
Is absolutely mind boggling
To me.
I'm sitting here listening to everything you want in a man,
He needs to be attractive, fit, financially stable, caring, generous, spontaneous
Intelligent, loyal, honest and I am nowhere near done with this list.
My question is, if this man that you so eloquently listed
Approached you right now, would you be ready?
Not just to be his arm candy and receive all the benefits that he can give,
Can you add to what he has?
I mean, truth to be told you're not fit…yet.
You haven't finished school…yet.
And you still live with mom.
WITH NO PLANS OF LEAVING.
When are you gonna become what you want to attract?
That's like trying to rent a penthouse when you can only afford a room.
We're supposed to bypass what you look like but uphold allll
These crazy expectations y'all put on us?
What kind of twisted power struggle y'all got going on?
Nah.
I'm supposed to just be happy that you picked me?
Nah.
Men won't say it because it'll hurt your feelings.
But I'm your brother and I can do that.
Before you go trying to bag someone that's out of your league at the moment
Why don't you at least reach the same playing field.

HEPROV: THE MONOLOGUE COLLECTION

LOVE WHO YOU LOVE

Stop calling me weak because I'm not with someone that looks like you
"I must hate the skin of my mother"
Do you even know my mother?
She raised a strong man that loves and respects all people.
I'm sorry you weren't raised that way.
I was taught to appreciate the differences of people and understand that all people are the same.
There is no superior group.
Only an unfortunate inferiority complex that has been placed on us by a higher echelon.
If I don't subscribe or believe their thoughts,
Why should I live my life as if I do?
In fear of being judged.
The love that I have is genuine,
And if I decide to wed someone of another culture,
It is because I decided to.
I was not brainwashed into a sect that forces me to hate who I see
When she looks like me.
You don't get this grief when you date someone who's not like me
You're actually congratulated.
When there are no difference between
Why can't it just be?

HEPROV: THE MONOLOGUE COLLECTION

SO YOU THOUGHT

The immaculate deception arrives when
You think you deserve for free,
What I worked my whole life for.
That because you're pretty,
That gives you carte blanche to have whatever I have.
The pick of the litter
The jackpot
The piece de resistance.
Little do you know, I suspected this from day one and have dealt with you in that capacity.
Every dinner, every gift, every trip was carefully documented.
Every photo erased because I knew we weren't going to work.
You wanted the lights, the fame, the aggravating irritant that is called the paparazzi.
Why?
Because your life is boring.
It's like a vacant lot that no one has the desire to look in, park in or dive in.
And because you have no ambition, goals or anything that would make you responsible for yourself
You latch your tentacles onto the first man that gives you attention.
I bet you planned our whole wedding in your mind.
Right down to the pretty little flower petals you thought you'd walk on.
Oh, sorry for you.
That will never come.
Until you can fashion yourself into the being that you want to attract,
You will forever remain the poor little engine that never could.

HEPROV: THE MONOLOGUE COLLECTION

THE SACRIFICE

I'm positive that I could have never been the father that you needed.
The lifestyle that I chose would only put you in grave danger.
Seeing but never being seen has kept me and you alive thus far.
At this time, this very moment.
Acknowledging that I am your father only puts your life in more danger than it ever has been before.
It doesn't help in any way.
NOW, those who have suspected throughout the years can
Come after you with all their force.
We've just skimmed the surface of people who seek to see my dead.
To see my head plunged into the Hudson never to be heard of again.
They can't wait
When that day finally draws near.
You have to understand
This is not how I wanted things to happen.
It is my job to protect you from those who wish to do you and me harm.
Even if that means staying away from you.

HEPROV: THE MONOLOGUE COLLECTION

TOO LITTLE, TOO LATE

All my life, I've had to work hard for your acceptance.
Went to the best schools,
Graduated top of my class.
I have a great job,
A wife, 2 children.
I've accomplished a whole lot in my life.
And still, I stand before you as a 12 year old little boy
Hoping you would give me one ounce of respect.
One ounce of love.
I didn't ask you to teach me how to run the streets.
To lie, to cheat and never trust anyone.
I needed a father.
To help me navigate
To help me grow.
Where was he?
The man who I saw once upon a time
SMILE.
What? I had to be 9?!
The last memories I have of you were laying on a couch.
Filthy and Drunk.
Staggering to find a belt because I didn't win at a card game.
I WAS 16!
I had to go through a lot just to get where I am today and still!
It's not enough.
What do you think you'd get from me?
Sympathy?
No. Gratitude.
If I stayed in that house one more day, I'd be behind bars.
Because of your untimely death.
But fortunately for you.
You beat me to it.

HEPROV: THE MONOLOGUE COLLECTION

GONE TOO SOON

I rushed to the hospital.
Gotta call telling me you were in labor.
I dropped everything.
Left my boring meeting to get here.
To be with you and meet our little baby girl.
I even had a police escort because I got stopped for speeding.
He felt sorry for me and drove in front.
Apparently, black lives do matter.
It took me 20 minutes to get to the front desk and 5 minutes for them to tell me you didn't make it.
Complications with a late pregnancy that wasn't for seen in the hundreds of ultrasounds and check-ups you had.
I'm sitting here trying to process what they're telling me at the same time realizing that I will never see you again.
I don't understand where to start.
My daughter will never meet her mother.
How I am gonna be a mother to our daughter?
I was struggling to figure out how to be a father.
My only comfort was that you would be here.
We were supposed to do this together.
I should've read those books when you told me to.
Should've went to those classes that I was too busy for.
Now. I get to do on the job training that I was never qualified for.
Did you know about this already?
Did you know you wouldn't make it?
Did I miss the prep you gave me because you already knew I was doing this alone?

HEPROV: THE MONOLOGUE COLLECTION

I'M READY

I brushed off your silence as peace and your
Tolerance as winning.
Little did I know you were slipping away from me and I didn't know it.
Too keep it 100
I played games.
Made up lies.
Caused you to feel insecure.
Talked to different women.
All the while knowing what I had.
You were the good girl.
You know, the one you eventually wanted forever with
But don't want anyone else to have.
You were mine and I couldn't let anyone have what was mine.
I gave you enough to make sure you stuck around all the while not realizing you were getting tired.
Those "Good Morning forehead kisses" turned into you just leaving.
When we would normally go back and forth on what to eat,
Sure became the broken record that now I'm dying to hear.
I took advantage one too many times.
When I decided to leave without an explanation,
I just knew I could come back just like before.
I tried calling you. No answer.
Tried to surprise you at your job.
You don't work there anymore.
Checked your social media.
They're all private and now I can't see what's going on.
I went to the doorman at your apartment.
They keep telling me you're not home.
But you can't be out ALL the time.
You gotta come home sometime, right?
I'll just sit and wait for you.
I know you'll want to finally hear that I'm sorry and I'm ready.
I just gotta catch you.
Cause now, you're just too busy

HEPROV: THE MONOLOGUE COLLECTION

STANDING IN ATTENTION

Oh how the tables have turned.
I've enlisted my counterpart- your
younger brother if you must know
To take your place.
I've waited 20 years for you to open your eyes to your value
But you'd rather waste your time
Following behind people, cleaning up their little diapers
All the while your life is in ruin and shambles.
When was the last time you said no?
I can tell you when.
NEVER.
Why?
Because for some ridiculous reason,
You feel or think you're the one they can trust.
That you will be praised and honored because you hid Massa's secrets!
As if you are their shining glory Mother Teresa.
When in fact, you are Harriet Tubman but you refuse to take your place.
The time of going with flow,
Wallowing in the tulips as the wind maneuvers your sundress
is over.
The time has come for you to get up off your laurels and lead your people to greener pastures by any means necessary.
Yes, you will anger them.
Yes they won't understand but it doesn't matter.
We have sat and watched them rule for centuries tearing us apart
Playing Daddy Warbucks with our money and our women.
And you,
Thinking you're safe taking a seat at their table
When you should be making your own.
Isn't your back tired?
Your fingers brittle?
Cause I'm sick of looking at you getting dirty

When given the chance
They'd turn their backs on you.

HEPROV: THE MONOLOGUE COLLECTION

HEPROV: THE MONOLOGUE COLLECTION

NO MORE BOY

I have sat here and allowed you to come between every relationship that I've had.
You don't like how she dresses.
She can't cook.
She looked at you wrong.
When all the while, you're afraid that I'm going to leave you.
I love you but Mom,
But I'm gonna leave.
It is my duty to leave.
I can no longer be the man of your house.
That was never supposed to be my job.
Instead of me learning how to be a man and grow into that,
I had to just know.
I started working to help pay bills when I should have been living as a teenager.
But did I complain?
No.
I sacrificed for us because I thought we needed it.
When come to find out, you were pocketing the money that dad gave to me once I finished college.
I never asked you for anything.
You mean to tell me that I finally bring someone home who I think is amazing and compassionate,
Who I finally think can meet you without be completely embarrassed,
You run her off because she doesn't sound or act like you?
I love you but you are bitter and wrong.
If you continue to berate the woman that I love,
You're gonna lose me.
And you will have no one to blame but yourself.

HEPROV: THE MONOLOGUE COLLECTION

PAUSE FOR A SECOND

How many times can I tell you I love you?
I don't care what people say or think about us!
I chose to fall in love with you because there is no other person I'd rather wake up to.
No other person I'd call when something happens.
I'm tired of hiding our relationship because our parents won't agree.
That's what makes us special.
Against all odds, we preserve.
We love.
(Pause)
What do you mean this is a mistake?
You love me right?
Cause I know I love you.
Neither of us signed up for the abuse but look how we've conquered it.
TOGETHER.
We are stronger when we're a unit.
When did this become too much?
When did you change?
You were all for it in the beginning?
I've gotten tired too.
What keeps me going is our love for each other.
This isn't a game Ana.
My parents aren't speaking to me.
My family is looking at me crazy.
My friends are-
And now you're telling me that its over because it's too much?
So all that I love you was something to say?
Something to do?
Waste my time.
Mess up my life!
I guess love doesn't conquer all.

HEPROV: THE MONOLOGUE COLLECTION

ODDBALL

It's hard growing up not being the most popular kid in high school.
The thought of having your own mind is like telling someone that you like
Ed Sheeran.
It just doesn't happen.
Every day, I get picked on because my pants aren't tight
And I don't know half of the rap songs that are out now.
And you know I can't dance.
I'd rather play Dungeons and dragons than basketball.
You think you had it tough.
Try getting peer pressured into having sex at 16 when all I want to do is graduate without getting a girl pregnant.
It's not like it was in your day.
My whole high school life can go down the drain by one text message.
If someone sends a mass text, it doesn't matter if it isn't true.
It's out there.
FOREVER.
Trying to defend yourself makes it worse.
When I'm in school, I keep my head down and try to finish the day
Without spitballs on the back of my neck.
Dad, your son
Is a geek.
I'm ok with it.
I think you should be too.
I'm sorry I'm not the star you'd thought I would be.
I can only be me.

HEPROV: THE MONOLOGUE COLLECTION

EQUAL WORK

I see what you're doing here.
I've sat here listening to you lecture me about how to do my job
When to think of it,
You want my position.
I kept trying to understand why I kept getting asked to help you
Close certain clients and show you the ropes.
This is a setup and you almost had me.
Just because you're a woman doesn't mean you automatically deserve what I worked for.
Unlike you, it was hard out here for me.
I didn't sleep my way to this level.
The work you skim over and take for granted,
I've had pulled countless all nighters to get them done.
And here you come, "Fight for my right to take someone's job because I'm a woman" and everything is supposed to drop.
We don't do that here.
We actually believe in merit.
So, if you think you're gonna slide right in doing
Half of the work you were doing before
And then think you're gonna get promoted.
You need to wake up.

HEPROV: THE MONOLOGUE COLLECTION

OPENLY TOXIC

You know, Nikki.
I knew something was going on.
I just wasn't sure.
I know I haven't been around,
Been extra busy.
I know I'm not the spontaneous type.
But we married for better or worse.
You bring some stranger into this marriage and you expect me to understand?
Would you be as understanding if the tables were turned?
I didn't think so.
What about our children?
He better not have been around them.
10 years, Nikki.
10 years.
I thought we got all the cheating out in the beginning.
At least that what you told me.
We both rushed in,
Did things that we both regretted.
Now you're telling me that you did it again?
I should punch-
Nope.
I said I wasn't gonna do that again.
This ain't a marriage.
We're roommates.
With children.
And you know what?
We're both over it.
What did you expect me to say?
Go ahead on seeing him?
You are definitely a piece of work.
It's…what time is it…11pm.
Pack your stuff and get out.
I'm sure your man will appreciate it.

HEPROV: THE MONOLOGUE COLLECTION

REVERSE ABUSE

I'm tired of being the punching bag when she gets mad.
I gotta hold her down so she won't hit me
Then I gotta keep my cool so I won't punch her in the face.
When did this become ok?
You can hit me, slap me
But I can't retaliate.
I know that's bad
I know I'm a dog for saying it.
But seriously.
If we're really being honest,
You wondered that too.
No one has the right to put hands on me if I can't defend myself.
Or at least hold them accountable.
I called the cops on my girl and told them she wailing on me.
You know what they did?
Came here asking her was she okay!
WHEN I CALLED THEM!
They walked me outside and couldn't believe that she's hitting and throwing things at me.
They actually laughed.
Yes, I said it.
They were laughing.
As if to say, why would I let this little girl hit me?
Well, if I hit her back then I'm going to jail.
No questions asked.
So I sit here and take it.
Like a punk.
Cause the bottom line is,
NO ONE is gonna believe me over her.

HEPROV: THE MONOLOGUE COLLECTION

SEE CLEARLY

There's so many struggles that I go through on a daily basis that I just chuck up to life.
To my dumb mistakes.
Even to immaturity.
I have never disrespected you.
Never put hands on you.
Never called you out your name.
I was a pretty stand up kind of guy.
This has to be the grimiest thing you have ever had done to me.
I know we've had our issues.
We've had some arguments.
Just answer this one question.
When have you ever feared for your life?
Don't you understand that as a black man dating a white woman
Those words can easily be the difference between life and death?!
At a moment's notice?!
One call to the cops and they're asking me to step outside...IN HANDCUFFS No questions asked.
They already see me as a threat and the minute you make their assumption a reality.
I'm done.
This is the last time you'll see me.
It's clear now,
Being with you, I have to fear for my life.
Look over my shoulder.
You really don't care.
I can almost bet,
You Never did.
It doesn't matter now.
I'm leaving before my life hangs in your hands.
Bethany,
Who's knocking at the door?

HEPROV: THE MONOLOGUE COLLECTION

JUDGE YE

Walking out my door, I'm a threat.
People cross the street
Clinch their purses when they see me.
Cause I'm a threat.
It's 7 in the morning and I'm just trying to get to work.
My first job.
Cause tuition costs.
Cops pull up next to my car.
Giving me the longest stare.
I just look forward.
No sudden moves.
Turn down my music.
I see them lurking
Needing a reason to pull me over.
So they can check my registration.
Yea its mine.
I should let them,
Just to see their agitation.
Walking around extra polite
Apparently people are afraid of me.
Didn't realize an unarmed man, walking down the street
Causes people to stay away from me.
Timbs, jeans and a t-shirt.
Construction is dirty.
Man, it doesn't matter
Its an excuse
They say.
He don't really work.
Little do they know, I own my home.
2 cars and a business.
They don't see the scars of life that birthed the man they see.
None of that matters, they already judging me.
You'll never understand or see my worth.
The real question is
Do you see your dirt?

HEPROV: THE MONOLOGUE COLLECTION

PLACE THE BLAME

Women wonder why I can't commit
It's not that I can't,
It just doesn't fit,
The lifestyle I've fashioned and come to be.
Not letting you ladies get that close to me.
When it all boils down half of you don't want a relationship.
You want someone to buy you things you know you can't afford.
The material is really all that you look for.
Meaningful conversation becomes a task
You're more concerned with Snapchat and Instagram filtered Ads.
You see, I had a relationship.
I was faithful to the tee.
Loyalty was no question, she had all of me.
She never had to want for nothing because I freely gave.
Wanting to know her in every way.
But she said I was too soft
Cause I like a picnic.
Why is that a problem?
I'm told old for FreakNic.
See, I'm convinced that women are all talk
Don't know what they really want.
A thug mixed in with sophistication.
Rough around the edges with a soft heart
Who ain't no punk.
That's 5 different dudes built into one.
What kind of schizophrenic mind control are you into?
When in reality you don't even know who you are
Stop looking for me to be everything you need,
When you won't find me a band aid if I bleed.
No I ain't soft.
Don't act like I'm tough
It's because of y'all
I blackened my heart.

HEPROV: THE MONOLOGUE COLLECTION

WE CAN'T HURT

I'm tired of going through the same thing over and over again.
The amount of time it takes for me to fix one situation another pops up.
I know what most people will say.
This is what I signed up for.
Being in the public, I have to have thick skin.
Ignore what everyone says.
Keep my headphones on.
But what I supposed to do when it hits my family.
They don't deserve this.
I paid for my mistakes.
For my shortcomings.
But the only thing people remember is what you did.
Not what you're doing.
I don't need to run down my accomplishments.
I know how I am.
The problem with society is that what makes for good TV.
Or good gossip
Is the downfall of others.
Preferably the ones with money.
Like I can't complain.
Can't be mad.
Just gotta play my part.
While you rip me and family to shreds.
I didn't tell ya'll to put me on a pedestal.
I just happen to make a lot of money.
When are we going to take responsibility to for own lives instead of trying to pin it on everyone else?

HEPROV: THE MONOLOGUE COLLECTION

ARE WE READY?

There are so many challenges in life that rock me to my core
But me as a man, it is my responsibility to keep going.
I don't have time to hurt or feel emotions.
It is my job to always have a plan
Women look to us for guidance.
But they don't really know the pressure.
Nor should they have to.
Time and after time,
We shift our responsibility to them because we're not ready.
Punk out, whatever you wanna call it.
Bottom line is,
How can we expect women to trust us when we don't trust ourselves?

HEPROV: THE MONOLOGUE COLLECTION

A DIFFERENT KIND

What is our problem?
What's the issue?
Every time we talk,
It turns into a screaming match.
You are so concerned with getting what you have to say out that you have yet to listen.
Then you belittle whatever I say because of course you're more important.
I'm tired of feeling like the dumb hunchback that you walk around with
As if I don't have a matter.
I may not be as aggressive than most
But I shouldn't have to be.
I shouldn't have to shake you and punch you in the face for you to know that I love you.
But that's not what you want.
You want someone to throw you all over the place,
Make you cry, make you feel less than.
Cause then in some twist way
That's love to you.
Well, I'm sorry.
You've picked the wrong man.
And I will not stoop to your level because you don't know what love is.

HEPROV: THE MONOLOGUE COLLECTION

PAY THE PIPER

You're a worthless piece of space.
The only reason why you are even in the position for you to be seen is because of me.
Remember when you needed someone to drop a little pill into Cinta's drink
And her voice somehow was hoarse?
Or when Teray accidentally tripped down the stairs
And she couldn't walk for 2 months?
You got your time to shine, remember.
That solo bug bit you and you didn't want it to stop.
You may not have said it to my face that you wanted those things to happen
But you sure didn't stop me.
And now, you became a household name and you think you don't owe me.
You actually think you got here based on pure talent.
Dana, you not that good.
In fact, you were the weakest.
You just happen to be prettier.
And all those people that's hanging around you now won't tell you that to your face.
But I will.
If you want your career to remain where it is,
You'll remember who got you there.

HEPROV: THE MONOLOGUE COLLECTION

MY PRECIOUS

Well would you look at here.
You finally decided to bring the boy I've been hearing so much about.
Son, do you know who I am?
I'm Christine's father.
That means I'm her provider, her confidant.
The man she comes running to when snotty little boys like you break her little heart.
I've molded her to become the confident articulate woman that she is today.
So if there is anything in your DNA that alerts you to the alarming fact that
You may hurt her in anyway,
I'd advise you to cut your losses immediately.
Because after I console her and remind her of what kind of woman she is because you've beaten her spirit and soul down to the point of no return,
I have to use my CIA antennas to find you in whatever sloven- filled ditch that you've ran to and remind you of this conversation in ways that your
little pea brain of a mind can comprehend.
Why do you think my daughter is happy?
Because she knows that I will come to her rescue
Any day, any hour and any lifetime.
Can you do the same?

HEPROV: THE MONOLOGUE COLLECTION

HEPROV: THE MONOLOGUE COLLECTION

SHADOW NO MORE

You know Dad,
I have done everything you have asked me to do.
And more.
I have literally mapped out my life to your plans
Just to make you happy.
What do you say?
Nothing.
You don't care that I'm walking in your footsteps and forgetting my own
Just for you to be proud of me.
I know you're not big on hugs or affection or anything that
Reminds you of a father actually loves me.
But it doesn't matter.
Cause I don't need it.
And I don't want it.
I love myself for the both of us and anyone else who doesn't believe in me.
I'm tired of walking in your shoes.
I have a whole life to live
And I refuse to let you guilt me into doing what you want me to do.
Because it's safe for you.
If you have any ounce of love for the son you brought into this world,
You may not like it.
But at least respect it.

HEPROV: THE MONOLOGUE COLLECTION

HEPROV: THE MONOLOGUE COLLECTION

TIME WASN'T OUR FRIEND

There's so much I thought we would be able to do.
More time I thought we would get.
I'm sitting here waiting for you to play some cruel joke on me.
I'm alive LJ!
But its been 10 minutes and you're really not breathing.
I didn't have the time before,
Now I'm realizing we didn't have enough.
There was always some show or some deal that came in between,
I feel like such a fool.
I treated the love of my life like she would never leave me side.
But I'm sitting.
ALONE.
Without you.
Why did you tell me your condition was this serious?
We would have done things so differently.
Cherished every moment
Like it was our last.
And now, all I can think of are the things I wanted to do with you
But never got the chance to.
I love you
At the same time, I'm sorry.
Sorry for not realizing that spending time with you was just as important as providing for you.
That focusing all of my time into creating a life diminished us living life.
There's nothing I can do to bring you back.
Nothing.

HEPROV: THE MONOLOGUE COLLECTION

OPEN SESAME

You know I'm not the open kind of guy.
Or emotional.
But it's something about you that makes me forget why I've always been that way.
Been trying to understand and figure it out but nothing comes to mind.
I feel whole.
At peace.
And there's nothing you can do to change the way I feel about you.
With you this feels normal.
Even though I've never done any of the things before.
You make me smile more
Or at all which is weird.
You somehow snuck into my life and turned on a fire that I didn't
Know was burned out.
I never want it to burn out.
As long as we do this together.
There's nothing we can't do.

HEPROV: THE MONOLOGUE COLLECTION

TRUE REALITY

So you stand before me wanting me to respect you?
You've taken it upon yourself to conjure up this self-righteous speech of entitled praise.
No, No, No.
Please, let me continue.
I sat here and listened to your wining and crying about your self-inflicted pain that you somehow decided was my fault.
Exactly when did you come up with that notion?
That all of the decisions in your life that you've made,
Especially the dumb mistakes, were contingent upon my love and respect for you.
You decided that the responsibility of you flunking out of school and getting arrested was not because you lack self-control but because daddy didn't kiss your boo-boos when you were a boy.
He didn't come to my game and that's why I have chosen to screw up my life.
If that isn't the most entitled, lackluster, immature, self-absorbed thought that you have ever decided to use.
And that's why you could never become the man you're supposed to be.
You're looking for affection when it's not needed.
This world is not going to coddle you and rub your bruises and tell you it's ok
The bad man is gone.
According to the world, you ARE the bad man.
And it's my job to get you ready for a world that doesn't want you here.
A world that if they had the chance would shoot you in the chest and call it self- defense if they knew they could get away with it.
But you don't want to understand that.
It's always rose-colored glasses and the blame game with you.
Whenever you are ready to decide to be a man and not this little boy, I'll be here, waiting.
As usual.

HEPROV: THE MONOLOGUE COLLECTION

IT'S NOT ALL OF US

Everyone tells us,
If you're not a bad cop,
Why don't you speak up?
I speak the truth,
Behind closed doors.
But how many really listen?
We all know what's going on here.
We do the best we can with what we've got.
It's the media's job to place all the blame on
EVERY SINGLE COP.
But it's us who make the decision to wake up in the morning and
Put on that uniform
Stare death in the face every time we enter a situation.
DESPITE what you think of us.
DESPITE what the media wants you to know.
We all know there's bad ones out there
Living La Vida Loca
Why should I use social media to show I'm doing my job?
I shouldn't have to parade me doing my job when stuff hits the fan.
But y'all expect me to.
Just so you'll determine I'm not a part of the problem.
Cause social media is soooo reliable.
When the actual problem is seeking validation because my fellow brothers decide to go left.

HEPROV: THE MONOLOGUE COLLECTION

WHEN IT HITS

Every man has his day of reckoning
Or coming to himself.
Sometimes it takes longer because it's taken longer to see the wrong.
There are dozens and dozens of women that deal with our crap
Because they think we love them.
When actually it's easier to give her what she wants then to find someone new.
It never fails,
It's the same some stuff.
We cheat. We lie. We steal.
We do literally everything possible to a woman but she will still be loyal.
That's a type of loyalty I don't ever want be.
That's the stuff that completely rids you of your intelligence and tells you that this person loves you anyway.
That the hurt and pain is just him acting out.
When has that EVER been the case?
We know what we want.
We know what we can get away with.
We'll even try a little more to see if there's a boundary.
We might think about consequences but it doesn't really sit.
We're people of now.
This mentality doesn't really change until we somehow get caught with someone that has the same thought process we do.
When we feel that crap.
The same way y'all did.
When we wanna kill the girl that broke our hearts.
That's the when the day of reckoning appears.
It never hits straight on.
Always in the back.
Why?
Cause we don't look that far.

HEPROV: THE MONOLOGUE COLLECTION

ODE TO CHANGE

It's hard from to say what I really want.
Cause I know I'm not ready for it.
I know I got a big mouth and I like to hear myself talk.
But that's my personality.
Hey, love it or hate it.
But what I cherish and want the most is also the scariest of them all,
Someone who sees past my antics.
Seems me at the core.
Who looks at my foolishness and ignores it because I'm being childish.
To be able to call me out
Without emasculating me.
Realizing that I'm in a sunken place of vacant stimulation and I just need to get it out.
No matter how dumb it sounds.
To know that it will never leave our safe haven,
The circle of trust.
She'll also causes me to revolutionize my thinking
To become stronger and not louder.
Seeing that I can no longer roll over
The invisible border
Cause I have to grow.
The question is,
Do I want to grow?
Do I want to part ways with the person I've been?
Starting with the excuses of sin?
To be held accountable for the venom I speak.
No longer the smartest person you see.
Could that really be me?

HEPROV: THE MONOLOGUE COLLECTION

DOCILE

The less I chose to ignore,
The more I need to grow.
The lack of true manhood that sweeps our nation
Still gives me an excuse to remain docile.
I will forever continue with the mantra
I'm doing the best I can with no real effort of
CHANGE.
The excuses I continue to give only fuel the desperate women to want
To change me.
Not understanding that if I wanted to change into the man I'm supposed to be,
I wouldn't need another "mommy" to walk me through it.
I'd just do it.
Countless times, I've watched women give me their best speeches of whatever they feel is my problem.
I don't have a problem.
I chose to stay clueless
Why?
I have no need to accept responsibility for my actions.
Simply because,
I don't want to.
I live my life on the basis of free will.
To remain incapable of ever giving you the love and affection you deserve all the while draining whatever love you think I need from you.
For my benefit.
If you give it, I will take it.
Don't expect to me morph into the person you think I should be when you should have accepted what I gave you...
In the beginning.

HEPROV: THE MONOLOGUE COLLECTION

HEPROV: THE MONOLOGUE COLLECTION

SAME TIME, SAME THING

You think I'm not judged based on what you see?
Every woman judges a man based on what he looks like
Regardless if she admits it or not.
She'll say she wants to get to know you, your looks aren't THAT important.
But trust and believe,
If your clothes aren't right,
Her friends are gonna hear.
What's the first thing women say after they've meant someone.
"Girl his body is nice!"
And you tell me women aren't visual creatures.
They give all this talk about men only looking at them for their bodies and not for their minds
When they do the same thing!
We're just supposed to bypass it because…you know.
WOMEN.
But we go through the same thing women do.
If not more because y'all look to us for safety.
Comfort. Relaxation.
If we can't give you that.
You're walking out the door.
Don't fight me because it's true.
To say that men aren't as conscious about their physical bodies as much as women is like saying there's only one product to glue a lace front.
It's just not true.

HEPROV: THE MONOLOGUE COLLECTION

LAPPY

Beloved,
Where do you think my love comes from?
I cook for you.
Clean for you.
Tell you everything you want to hear.
Am I not supposed to drown you with every piece of love you desire?
This is what you wanted.
For me to be everything you wanted me to be.
To rid myself of all of things that you didn't like
Just so you could love me.
You don't like what you see?
Well, that's how it feels when you constantly try to fix me.
To manipulate me into seeing things your way.
ALL DAY.
The fact that you don't want your man to have an opinion says a lot about the kind of men you normally come in contact with.
You like to be the driver.
You don't want a man,
You want a lap dog.
Someone to run up behind you and sniff your leg.
Tell you how pretty you are when you should already know that.
Someone to kiss your feet as you kick them in the face.
Keeping them beat down and subservient.
Well I ain't no punk
And I ain't doing that.

HEPROV: THE MONOLOGUE COLLECTION

CHAINS THAT BIND ME

Have you ever wondered what it would be like?
If we got divorced?
You don't like me, I don't like you.
Even the kids can see that something is definitely wrong.
When did we get to the point of no return?
Where we don't ever try anymore.
Is our love that sour?
Our union that broken?
We've been so busy taking care of the family,
We forgot the core people.
And now we can't stand the sight of each other.
We no longer know each other
We're starving bone dry
With no energy to water.
The one place that needed refreshing the most.
Now all I can feel is the heavy chains that latch onto me
As I step in this house.
The light that normally lifts my mood serves as a spotlight to my wrongdoing
Whatever it is that day.
We stopped trying
We stopped caring.
We grew…we changed and we managed to distance ourselves from the one person that kept us united.
There's no need to fight the inevitable.
What we both know we need.
After 20 years of love,
It's time to heed.

HEPROV: THE MONOLOGUE COLLECTION

IT AIN'T REAL

I worked hard for this.
Broke my arm for this.
Knew this was the only way to take care of my family.
So I focused all my energy into making it.
Sacrificed friends, parties, girls.
Cause I knew there was a big plan at stake.
Went through high school figured out a way to remain an honor academic.
While maintaining my stride as an athlete.
Nothing was holding me down.
No one could stop be.
My time has finally come.
I decided to enter the draft right out of high school.
Something I probably should not have done.
The pressures of living life and taking care of the family got to me.
I even stepped to my dad, but he reminded me quick to the real man of the house.
Shot out to em.
I have everything and everyone telling me, advising me, almost near forcing me to their plan.
They don't bother to ask me.
As if I'm dumb.
Like I didn't work to get where I am.
It's all fun and games til they see dollar signs.
Then everyone reminds you of your place.
When in all actuality I'm the only one that knows what's at stake.
Now, I'm sitting here with a broken arm and and torn knee.
You'd think one of the would've came to see about me.

HEPROV: THE MONOLOGUE COLLECTION

THE ONLY ONE

My parents put me in this school.
To get a better education.
But all I keep getting are smirks and stares.
You would think being 2018, I wouldn't have to deal with this.
But this is a private school
Everything happens here.
I keep getting asked if I'm gonna basketball.
Sidebar, I don't even like basketball.
I know I'm supposed to appreciate where I am.
But how can I when everything is so weird.
I try to stay neutral on issue during class.
But I get the task of blacksplaining everything
As if they'd understand.
Still and yet, I'm supposed to sit here and be grateful.
I better not complain.
The token black boy with the great education.

HEPROV: THE MONOLOGUE COLLECTION

REMINISCE TO REVOLT

What happened to the days when I was able to walk the streets and
not be completely humiliated as a man?
To not have police circle around blocks because of who I am.
To have them shame me because I look like a regular dude.
Not even scared for fear of being sued.
Cause the last time I checked,
It's an all out war
With no one coming to our rescue.
We seized, We fight, We die.
Stay quiet, No longer a giant, We live.
What better way die
When we became the status quo?
When it's popular to hide behind your walls
Instead of meeting them at the door.
Too long have we remained calm while our brothers and sisters
Died
For the wrong reasons.
When no real justice was given.
I'm tired of giving out excuses and chances to people that have no
intention of learning and changing the behaviors of their past.
It's too comfortable, it's easier to last.
It's time for us to get up and unite.
Be the next generation
Ready to fight.
Come soon, Come never
We have the might.
To put them in their place for all to take flight.

HEPROV: THE MONOLOGUE COLLECTION

TIRED YET?

When we hold ourselves accountable to the actions of our brothers.
Only then can we unite.
If we don't look after our people,
We will drag each other into the ground.
By choice.
There is nothing more meaningful,
Nothing more powerful than strength.
And we lack so much of it.
We stand on our individual convoluted soapboxes
As if we are right
And we have the nerve to get mad at Kanye's plight.
We've become so forward and free that we have allowed wrong thinking to equal evolution.
When it should be stopped in its track and educated.
But we don't have time for that.
We're too busy in our own mental slavery to money and looking successful to people we don't even know.
Our priorities are no longer help
your brother.
Nothing is no longer sacred.
When do we get to the place of enough?

HEPROV: THE MONOLOGUE COLLECTION

REMEMBERING YOUR PLACE

Your voice will never overpower mine.
You think because I allowed you to go to some women's group that
Gives you the right to start speaking as if you forgot your place in this house?
I shouldn't have to continuously remind you who's head of this house.
Everything stops with me.
You don't go anywhere unless you ask me.
You don't buy anything unless you ask me.
And you don't dress unless I approve.
This is nothing knew.
We have not changed.
Our duties are still the same.
Your job is to take care of the children and cook.
You don't even have to clean
I mean you're not good at it anyway
But think of the rest you get for not having to do that.
There are plenty of women that would kill to be in your position.
To not have to work.
I wish you wouldn't be so ungrateful.
It's not becoming.

HEPROV: THE MONOLOGUE COLLECTION

MAMA'S BOY BREAKUP

You used to make my day when you came home.
Now I'd rather not be home.
There's no real or comfortable way to say this.
So, I'm just gonna say it.
I don't want this.
This has become too much of a chore.
It's no longer fun.
I feel like one of your children.
I've tried talking to you.
I've tried staying away from you.
Whatever I do turns out wrong.
You say you want this to work
But do you really?
I don't think you even believe that.
I'm gonna go stay with my mom.
She already knows what's going on.
I didn't mean to spring this one you.
I hope we can be friends?

HEPROV: THE MONOLOGUE COLLECTION

ROLE REVERSAL

Man, I would feel great if my wife made my money than me.
I could finally be the stay at home dad I've always wanted to be.
I'm definitely the nurturer in this family and it would honestly do our kids some good.
Why do you keep telling me that my wife is going regret me staying home?
Who cares!
Can I get something out of this marriage?
She's always been the go getter type.
Always on the go.
Doing 100 million different things at one.
You know that.
I can't do all of that.
My brain isn't that fast.
I appreciate the calm in life.
She stay running in here crazy ruining dinner
Because she's always late.
What's the big deal if we changed roles for the sake of our family?
Do we really need society to tell us how to be?

HEPROV: THE MONOLOGUE COLLECTION

HIDING

I'm sorry that I took advantage of you.
Left you at the most vulnerable and crucial time of your life.
I wasn't the man you needed me to be and I'm sorry.
I caused you to remain hurt for 10 years.
And I understand that.
It's all my fault, Rayna.
Mine.
Not my family.
They don't deserve this.
I'll say it.
I knew he raped you.
I knew the minute you told me.
I said nothing.
I allowed people to ridicule you, ostracize you.
I allowed you to think it was all in your head because I was too weak to stand by your side.
Too afraid of what everyone else would be thinking.
If there was any way that I could go back in time and do this all over again,
I would be right by side like you needed me to be.
You were there for me through it all.
I dropped the ball big time.
Just leave me family out of this.
It's just me and you.
We can go to the police together and talk this out.
We can get him together.
Just please put the gun down.
I begging you
Rayn-!

HEPROV: THE MONOLOGUE COLLECTION

OLD FAMILY

Mom!
What are you talking about I'm not your biological son?
What does that even mean?
Why is he saying that I was adopted?
This can't be true!
(Pause)
All this time you knew I was adopted and you just decided not to tell me?
You didn't think I needed to know that.
I should not have found out I had a whole different family by you getting sick.
You've kept this secret for my entire life and who knows if my real parents are even alive.
This is just another one of your selfish acts that AFFECT EVERYONE.
Do I have any siblings?
Do they live in town?
Do you know them?
My whole life is a complete lie and you can't even fix your mouth to say sorry.
What kind of person does this?
Who are you right now?

HEPROV: THE MONOLOGUE COLLECTION

We can only be happy when you become our true selves

www.ingramcontent.com/pod-product-compliance
Lightning Source LLC
Chambersburg PA
CBHW060529010526
44110CB00052B/2544